History in

ROMAN BRITAIN

Martin O'Connell

Wayland

History in Evidence

Cover design: Alison Anholt-White
Series design: Helen White
Consultant: Barry L Marsden

Cover pictures: The main picture is part of a floor mosaic at the palace at Fishbourne, in West Sussex. The inset is a gold Roman coin.

First published in 1989 by
Wayland (Publishers) Limited
61 Western Road, Hove
East Sussex BN3 1JD, England

© Copyright 1989 Wayland (Publishers) Limited

British Library Cataloguing in Publication Data
O'Connell, Martin.
  Roman Britain.
  1. England. Roman Empire civilisation
  I. Title II. Series
  936.2'04

HARDBACK ISBN 1–85210–574–7

PAPERBACK ISBN 0–7502–0541–5

Edited and typeset by Kudos, Hove, East Sussex
Printed in Italy by G. Canale & C.S.p.A., Turin
Bound in France by A.G.M.

Publishers' note
The publishers apologize for the following errors which appear in this book:

Page 16 In the diagram of the hypocaust, the arrangement of the round tiles shown is incorrect. The floor above the tile pillars normally consisted of concrete on top of a layer of flat tiles.

Page 22 The clay vase is of prehistoric origin (Early Bronze Age).

Page 23 The jar illustrated was used as a container for the cremated remains of a dead person.

Picture acknowledgements
The publishers wish to thank the following for permission to reproduce their illustrations on the pages mentioned: Aerofilms 5, 24; Janet & Colin Bord 12; C. M. Dixon/Photoresources 9 (upper), 21 (lower), 25, 28, 29; Michael Holford *cover*, 7 (upper), 9 (lower), 27; Ronald Sheridan/The Ancient Art & Architecture Collection 18; TOPHAM *cover inset*, 7 (lower), 8, 15, 17, 21 (upper). The remaining pictures are from the Wayland Picture Library. The artwork was supplied by: Malcolm S. Walker 4, 10-11, 16, 19, 25, 26, 27; Stephen Wheele 6, 12, 13, 14, 15, 17, 20, 29.

Contents

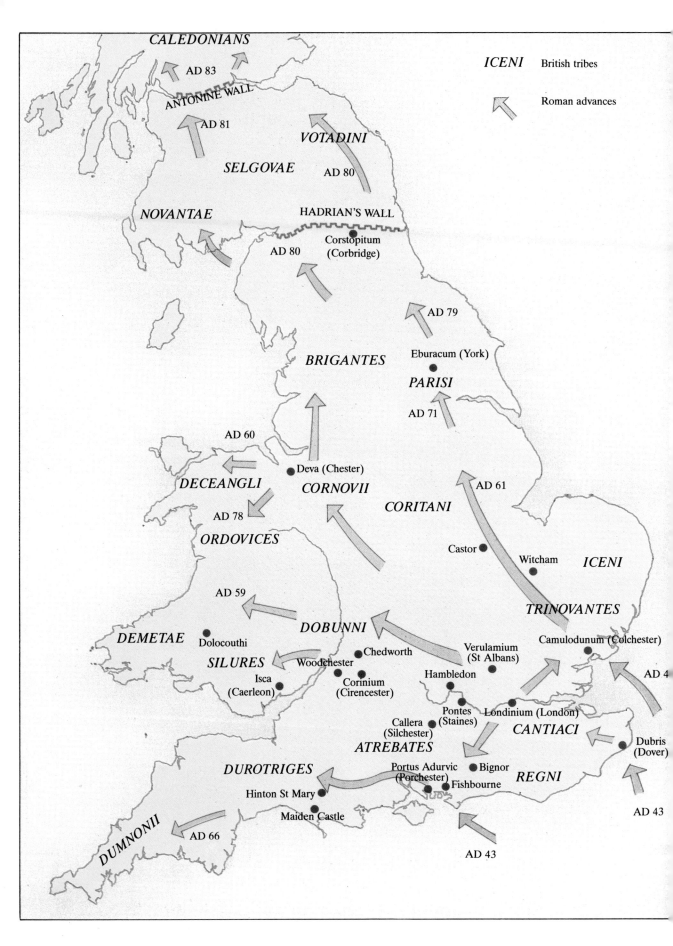

CALEDONIANS

AD 83

ANTONINE WALL

ICENI   British tribes

Roman advances

AD 81

VOTADINI

SELGOVAE

AD 80

NOVANTAE

HADRIAN'S WALL

Corstopitum
(Corbridge)

AD 80

AD 79

Eburacum (York)

BRIGANTES

PARISI

AD 71

AD 60

Deva (Chester)

DECEANGLI

CORNOVII

CORITANI

AD 78

ORDOVICES

AD 61

Castor

Witcham   ICENI

AD 59

DEMETAE

Dolocouthi

DOBUNNI

Camulodunum (Colchester)

SILURES

Chedworth

Verulamium
(St Albans)

TRINOVANTES

Woodchester

Isca
(Caerleon)

Corinium
(Cirencester)

Hambledon

Londinium (London)

AD 4

Pontes
(Staines)

CANTIACI

Callera
(Silchester)

ATREBATES

Dubris
(Dover)

DUROTRIGES

Portus Adurvic
(Porchester)

Bignor

Hinton St Mary

Fishbourne

REGNI

Maiden Castle

DUMNONII   AD 66

AD 43

AD 43

Invasion

The Romans built up a large empire over several centuries, which included most of Europe and the land around the Mediterranean Sea. The countries ruled from Rome were known as provinces. Britain became a province after the Roman Army invaded it in AD 43.

At that time, Britain was divided up into many tribes, most of whom were often at war with one another. Although groups of tribes in the south-east joined together to fight the Romans, they were quickly defeated. Some tribes, like those in the south-west, lived in fortified villages on high ground, known as hillforts. Excavations by archaeologists at one of these, Maiden Castle in Dorset, have shown how it was captured by the Romans. They used a *ballista* (a huge crossbow which fired iron bolts with wooden shafts) when they attacked the fort. The archaeologists found a cemetery of Britons who died during the battle for the hillfort, which contained male and female skeletons. One of these skeletons still had a *ballista* bolt stuck in its spine.

Although much of England and Wales, and parts of Scotland, were conquered, many tribes continued to rebel against the Romans while they were in Britain.

LEFT Here are the routes the Romans took to conquer Britain. All the places mentioned in this book are on this map, too.

Important dates	
55 BC	Julius Caesar's first invasion of Britain.
54 BC	Caesar's second invasion.
AD 43	Emperor Claudius's army landed in Britain.
60	Queen Boudicca led the Iceni tribe in a rebellion against the Romans.
122	Emperor Hadrian visited Britain and ordered his generals to build a wall along the northern edge of Roman land.
197	Northern tribes took over Hadrian's Wall, but the Romans recaptured it.
367	Hadrian's Wall was badly damaged by the Picts from Scotland.
383	A large part of the Roman Army left Britain.
407	Almost all the rest of the Roman Army left Britain.
410	The Romans left Hadrian's Wall and Britain is no longer ruled by Rome.

ABOVE Maiden Castle, in Dorset.

The Roman soldier

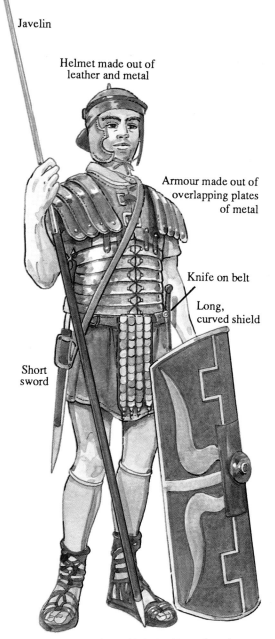

Javelin

Helmet made out of leather and metal

Armour made out of overlapping plates of metal

Knife on belt

Long, curved shield

Short sword

Leather sandals with hobnails on the soles

Here is a soldier ready to go into battle.

Legions made up the main part of the Roman Army that invaded Britain. Each legion had 5,300 heavily armed and well-trained foot-soldiers who, by law, had to be citizens of Rome. We know what these soldiers wore because pieces of their armour have been discovered at many excavations, including sites in Colchester (called Camulodunum by the Romans) and London (named Londinium). Some of the best examples of Roman armour have been found at Corbridge (Corstopitum), a fort in the north of England.

At the end of the first century AD, a typical soldier wore a uniform like the soldier in the picture on the left. On his feet he wore leather sandals with thick soles that had hobnails in them. The top of his body was protected by strips of metal, held together with leather, which fastened at the front with buckles and laces. The soldier wore a bronze helmet, which was strengthened with iron, and carried a long, curved shield. His weapons included a short, wide sword, a dagger and two throwing spears, each over 2 m long.

Alongside the legions were the 'auxiliary' regiments. These were made up of either 500 or 1,000 men. They were not citizens of Rome, but belonged to the countries Rome had conquered and now fought for her in foreign lands. These soldiers wore armour made of mail, or shirts which had overlapping metal scales. Their shields were smaller than the legionaries' ones and flatter, being either oval or six-sided in shape. Their helmets could be very fancy, like the beautiful one which has been discovered at Witcham, in Cambridgeshire.

RIGHT This piece of Roman armour was found in the north of England. It shows the overlapping 'scales' of metal that were designed to protect a soldier in battle.

BELOW Here is a group of people who meet regularly to re-enact Roman battles. Their uniforms and weapons are exact copies of Roman ones.

Forts and camps

Camps were temporary fortifications, put up at the end of a day's march. Each soldier in a legion carried a pickaxe and two stakes. He would use the pickaxe to dig a ditch around the camp, throwing up the earth to form a bank. When the ditch had been completed, all the men would stick their stakes into the top of the bank, forming a wooden wall. In the morning, the soldiers took their stakes with them, but did not fill in the ditch. Today, these ditches can be seen on hillsides in Wales and Scotland.

Forts were permanent bases for the Roman Army. The largest ones, called fortresses, were for the legions. As a result of archaeological excavations, we know that most of the fortresses were built in the same way. Caerleon (called Isca by the Romans) in Gwent is one of the best examples. It was designed to hold over 5,000 men, and it covered about 20 hectares of land. It was oblong in shape, with a gateway in each of its four sides, and surrounded by a ditch.

The legion's headquarters was situated at the point where the two main streets met. Behind it was the splendid home of the commander of the legion. Smaller houses for the senior officers were built

This is a reconstruction of the fort at Vindolanda, in Northumberland.

This picture shows the bastions in the walls of the fort at Porchester, in Hampshire.

near the main street. Other important buildings included workshops, baths and a hospital. The soldiers lived in long, narrow barracks, which had rooms at one end for the junior officers.

To start with, Caerleon was built in wood and probably looked like the fort that has recently been reconstructed near Coventry. Caerleon was rebuilt in stone at the end of the first century AD.

About two hundred years later, a new type of fort, again made out of stone, was built by the Romans to protect the eastern and southern coasts from attacking Saxons. Today, the best example of one of these is Portchester (Portus Adurni). It is famous for the towers, called bastions, sticking out of its walls.

All fortresses had their own hospital where doctors would have used instruments like these to treat sick soldiers. The box on the left held drugs and the metal jug caught blood that dripped from a wound.

Hadrian's Wall

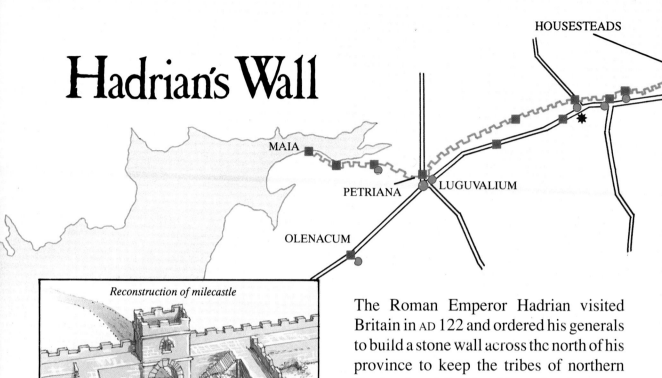

MAIA

PETRIANA   LUGUVALIUM

OLENACUM

HOUSESTEADS

Reconstruction of milecastle

The Roman Emperor Hadrian visited Britain in AD 122 and ordered his generals to build a stone wall across the north of his province to keep the tribes of northern England and Scotland in order. It was to stretch for nearly 120 km from the River Tyne, on the east coast, to the Solway Firth, on the west. Along it were forts, milecastles (small forts built exactly one Roman mile apart) and turrets.

Large parts of the wall still stand and we know what the missing pieces would have looked like from archaeologists'

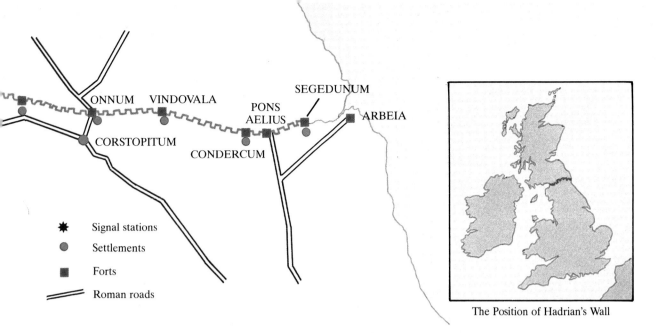

ONNUM
VINDOVALA
SEGEDUNUM
PONS AELIUS
CORSTOPITUM
CONDERCUM
ARBEIA

✳ Signal stations
● Settlements
■ Forts
══ Roman roads

The Position of Hadrian's Wall

discoveries. It was 6 m high and 3 m across at its widest point. There was a ditch in front and a large, flat-bottomed one with a mound on either side, called the *vallum*, behind it. Behind the wall a road was built later for the soldiers to use, along which supplies could be brought. Fortresses, like the one excavated at Housesteads (Borcovicium), were added on to the wall after it had been finished.

Housesteads fortress is very similar to Caerleon, only much smaller. At its centre were the headquarters building, the commander's house, granaries and a hospital. Next to them were the barracks for up to 1,000 auxiliary soldiers. One of the most interesting discoveries has been the lavatories, which once had wooden seats for twenty men at a time.

Over the years, traders set up businesses next to the fortress. Slowly, a small town developed, complete with temples, shops and houses. Soldiers' wives and families probably lived there, along with old legionary soldiers whose fighting days were over.

Cross-section of Hadrian's Wall

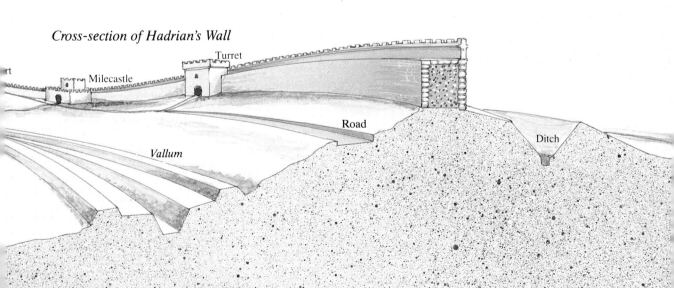

Turret
Milecastle
Road
Ditch
Vallum

Towns

Most Roman towns have been built over many times. The Roman remains can lie some 6 or 7 m below the surface. Silchester (called Calleva) in Hampshire has never been built on, so you can still see the town's walls, though nothing of the buildings can be seen.

Silchester provides us with a good idea of what a Roman town looked like. It was divided up into several rectangular blocks by rows of streets. At its centre was the *forum*, or market-place, where most of the

RIGHT The remains of the town walls of Caerwent. BELOW A plan of Caerwent.

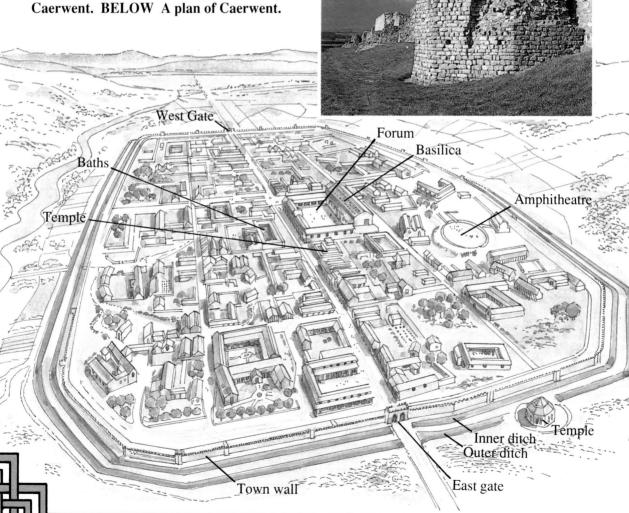

West Gate

Forum

Basilica

Baths

Amphitheatre

Temple

Temple

Inner ditch
Outer ditch

Town wall

East gate

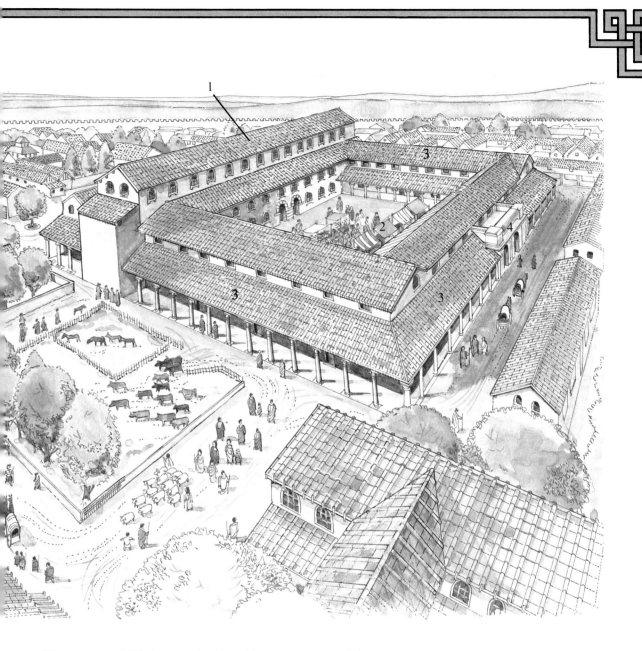

The centre of Silchester: *basilica* (**1**); *market stalls* (**2**); *forum* (**3**); **entrance to** *forum* (**4**).

businesses were situated. The *basilica* was joined to the *forum*. It contained the government offices, as well as law courts.

In the streets close to the *forum*, there were shops where craftsmen, like leather workers and silversmiths, worked and sold their goods.

Roman place names
Towns and cities with *porta* (meaning 'gate') and *castra* (meaning 'fort') in their names were places where the Romans settled: for example, Portsmouth, Portland, Lancaster and Doncaster.

Roman London

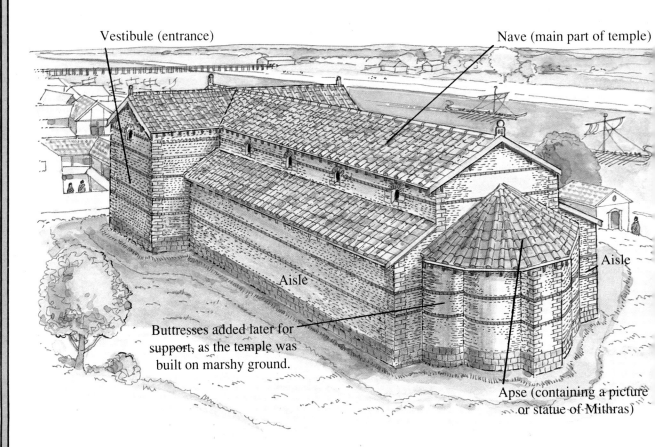

Vestibule (entrance)

Nave (main part of temple)

Aisle

Aisle

Buttresses added later for support, as the temple was built on marshy ground.

Apse (containing a picture or statue of Mithras)

The temple in London for worshipping the god Mithras looked like this.

Archaeologists now know that London was not only the capital of Roman Britain, but also an important trading place. Like other cities built by the Romans, much information has been destroyed in later years by rebuilding work. However, when the ground is being prepared for new buildings, Roman remains have often come to light, which archaeologists have then excavated for information.

In recent times, they have examined docks with wooden quays and storehouses along the bank of the River Thames between the Tower of London and London Bridge. They have also found what may be part of the Roman bridge across the river, which is very near the present London Bridge. The outline of a very

large *forum* and *basilica* have been discovered near the centre of the City of London, as well as the remains of a palace, which was probably the home of the Roman Governor of Britain. Other important discoveries include public baths, a pagan temple and an amphitheatre.

In the early part of the second century, a small fort was built in the north-east of Roman London, according to archaeologists who discovered its remains in 1947. Later on, at the beginning of the third century, a stone wall, connected to the fort, was built. When completed, the wall enclosed the city.

ABOVE Excavating a Roman wall in London.   BELOW London during Roman times.

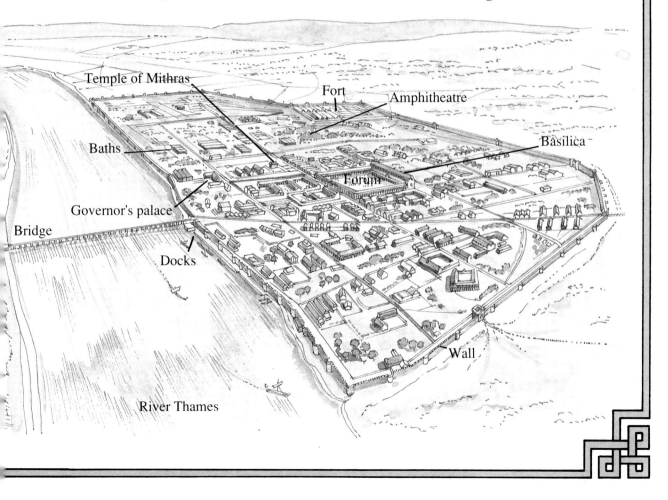

Villas

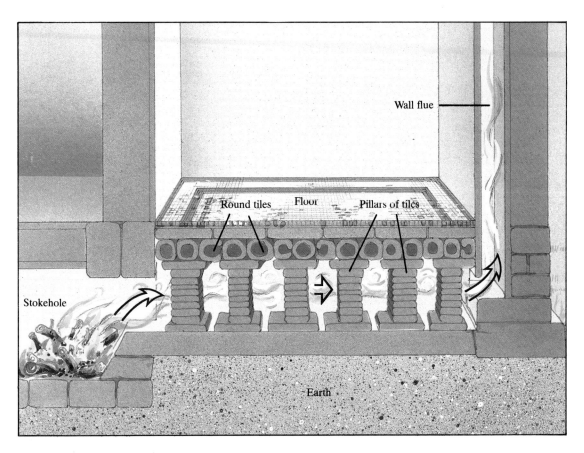

Labels on diagram: Wall flue, Round tiles, Floor, Pillars of tiles, Stokehole, Earth

This diagram shows how a hypocaust (a system of underfloor heating) worked.

'Villa' is a Roman word archaeologists use to describe the country houses of farmers or owners of land. Many villas probably started off as small houses with a few rooms. Afterwards, many of them had extra rooms added on to each end. Some villas were even knocked down and very large buildings with many rooms put up in their place.

In the fourth century, many villas, like the ones at Bignor, Woodchester and Chedworth, were completely rebuilt with a large number of rooms grouped around a courtyard. The rooms had beautifully painted walls and underfloor heating (see the diagram above). There were mosaics on the floors of the main rooms. These villas even had their own bath-houses.

Their owners must have been very rich or perhaps, as some people say, they were the home of several families.

Much bigger than these villas is the palace at Fishbourne, in West Sussex. It was built around AD 70 and was discovered in 1960 by some workmen who were digging trenches for drains. The palace had many rooms and courtyards arranged around a beautiful garden. The rooms inside the palace were decorated with magnificent mosaics, painted walls and ornaments brought from other parts of the Roman Empire. The palace probably belonged to Cogidubnus, leader of a local tribe of Britons. The Romans gave it to him as a reward for his friendship and support in times of trouble.

ABOVE Restoring a mosaic at Lullingstone.

BELOW A typical villa at Lullingstone, Kent.

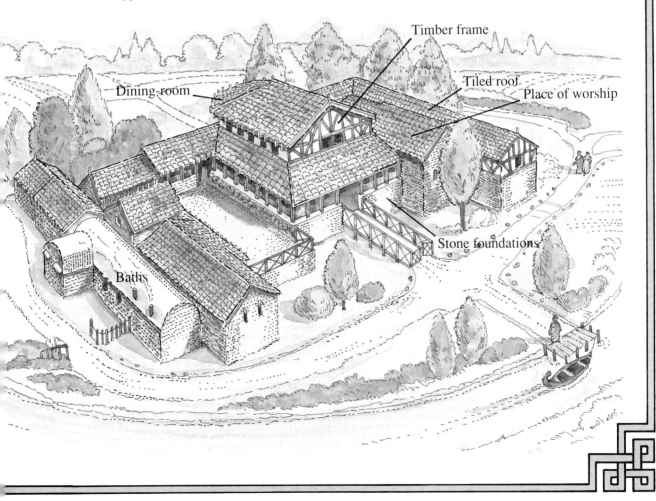

Timber frame

Tiled roof

Place of worship

Dining-room

Stone foundations

Baths

Farming

The remains of the granary at Housesteads fort. The stone pillars supported the floor and allowed hot air to circulate underneath it to dry the grain.

British farmers did not change their ways greatly with the arrival of the Romans, although the Romans' better-made equipment helped them to increase the size of their harvests.

Corn continued to be the most important crop, but farmers now had to grow more of it because they were expected to supply the Roman Army, as well as the people who lived in the cities.

The corn had to be dried before being stored for winter, otherwise it would have rotted. The Romans built special ovens for this purpose. The remains of one have been found at Hambledon, in Buckinghamshire. These ovens worked in the same way as the underfloor-heating systems in the Romans' town houses and villas. A furnace supplied hot air, which was then taken through channels below the floor.

Photographs taken from the air can show us what the ground below was once used for. Ditches and stone walls can be spotted from the air by the way crops grow over them. They grow taller and stronger over ditches, where the soil is deeper and richer. It is not so deep over walls, so the crops are shorter and weaker.

Bumps and dips in the soil produce shadows when the sun is low in the sky, in the early morning or late afternoon. These are best seen from the air, where the patterns they make are much clearer.

Stones from ancient buildings in the soil can be brought to the surface by ploughing. The patterns they produce can show the outline of a building.

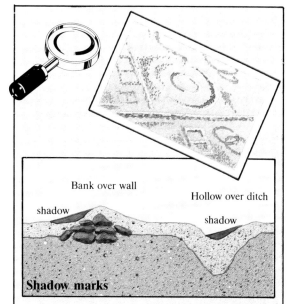

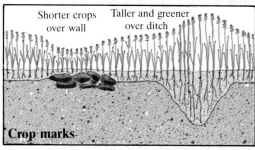

Bank over wall

Hollow over ditch

shadow

shadow

Shadow marks

Shorter crops over wall

Taller and greener over ditch

Crop marks

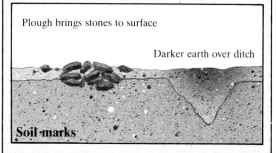

Plough brings stones to surface

Darker earth over ditch

Soil marks

Pictures from the air
Photographs taken from planes can show signs of ancient remains both above and below the ground. Three types of marks show up on the photographs: crop marks, soil marks and shadow marks.

Leisure

The main places for entertainment were the amphitheatres. Most of these were similar to the one that has been unearthed at Cirencester (called Corinium), which was built in the shape of an oval, surrounded with tiers of seats on an earth bank. The banks were often strengthened later by stone walls. The shows in the amphitheatre were often blood-thirsty ones. Armed men, called gladiators, would fight, sometimes to their death. Wild beast fights were also popular.

There were few theatres. Today, archaeologists think that most of them were used for religious ceremonies rather than for stage plays. A good example of a theatre has been excavated at St Albans (called Verulamium). To begin with, it was a cross between a theatre and an amphitheatre. The central area, called the

The theatre at St Albans, surrounded by a high wall with tiered seats for the audience.

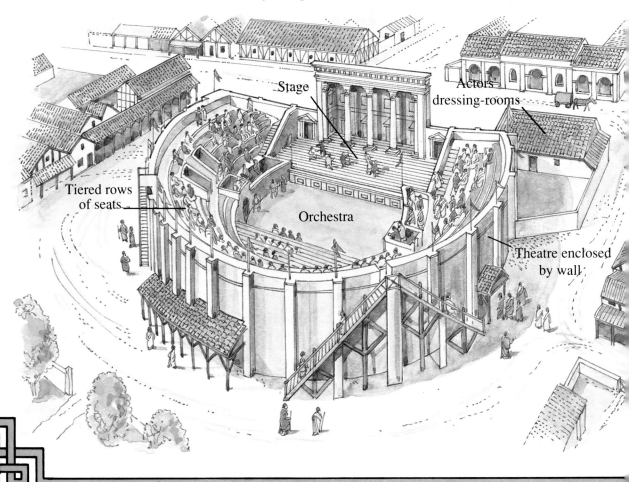

Stage

Actors dressing-rooms

Tiered rows of seats

Orchestra

Theatre enclosed by wall

These grassy banks hide the stone foundations of the amphitheatre at Caerleon.

orchestra, was circular and surrounded by tiers of seats, with a small stage at one end. Later, the stage was made much bigger and the orchestra made smaller. Like amphitheatres, theatres were open to the sky.

The public baths found in many towns and cities were places to meet friends and not just for washing yourself. At Silchester, the baths had an exercise area, dressing-rooms and lavatories. The baths themselves consisted of three rooms at different temperatures – cold, warm and hot. The bather would begin in the cold room and go on to the hottest one, where he or she would scrape off any remaining dirt with a curved instrument, called a *strigil*, before returning through the rooms in reverse order. Then the person would rub oil on to their body.

A view of one of the most famous and best-preserved Roman remains in Britain: the baths after which Bath is named.

Clothes and food

ABOVE This preserved leather shoe was found by archaeologists in excavations in London. Leather is a material which can survive well in damp places.

Only tiny pieces of clothing have survived since Roman times, because most material falls apart over the years. So, to know what people wore in Roman Britain, we have to rely on statues, and tombstones which have pictures of the dead carved on them.

For everyday use, most men wore a knee-length tunic with either long or short sleeves. Cloaks, fastened at the shoulder with a brooch, were also worn. They varied in length and were sometimes fitted with a hood. The *toga* was not easy to wear, so it was probably put on only for important occasions.

Women also wore tunics of varying

ABOVE A clay vase which has been carefully pieced together for display in a museum.

This ladle was once used to serve food and liquids at meal-times. It belonged to a wealthy Roman family and would have been used by one of their slaves.

ABOVE Archaeologists have unearthed this storage jar in which a Roman family would have kept grain.

lengths, judging from the pictures on tombstones found at York (called Eburacum) and Chester (Deva). Rich people had very beautiful tunics, made out of good-quality materials; poorer people had to make theirs out of cheaper, rougher fabrics.

Leather can survive very well in damp places. As a result, leather boots and sandals have been discovered at several places, especially in London.

Soil, containing a lot of water, also helps to preserve the remains of food, such as bones and seeds. By studying them, archaeologists can tell us what was eaten in Roman Britain. Now we know that beef was the most popular meat dish. Venison (from deer), chickens, small birds, fish (including shellfish, like oysters) were also eaten by people. A lot of herbs were used in the cooking of all this food. Vegetables and fruit were eaten at meals, and people drank wine and beer.

Roads

This is Stony Stratford, in Buckinghamshire, which lies either side of Watling Street.

The first roads were built by the Roman Army to connect all its forts together. Later, roads were made to join up all the towns and cities.   All these roads were as straight as possible so that people, animals and vehicles, like chariots and carts, could travel quickly from one place to another. Some of our modern roads actually lie on top of Roman ones, like the A5 north of St Albans.

The Romans built very wide roads, sometimes as much as 15 m across. Near the villa at Bignor, in West Sussex, arch-aeologists have found one which was 9 m wide, and made out of layers of chalk and flint 1 m deep.

Milestones were placed along the route to tell travellers how far they were from their destination. The Romans kept their roads in very good condition, repairing them frequently.

RIGHT This map shows the routes of the main roads built by the Romans.

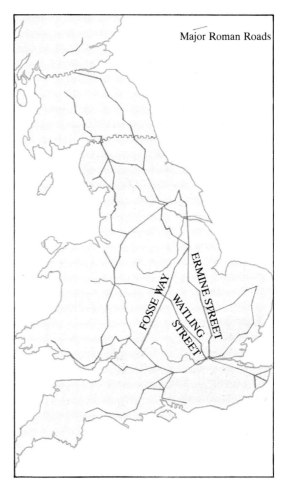

Major Roman Roads

FOSSE WAY

ERMINE STREET

WATLING STREET

Small towns often grew up at important points along these roads and farmers would come to them to buy and sell their goods. Staines (called Pontes) in Surrey is an example of one of these. It developed at the point where the road from London to Silchester crossed the Thames.

LEFT These are the remains of a Roman road across Wheeldale Moor, in Yorkshire. You can see that it was built as straight as possible so that travellers could reach their destination quickly.

Trade and industry

The Romans brought goods from all over their empire to Britain. Here are some of the goods found at archaeological sites: shiny bowls and plates from France; large pottery containers for olive oil (called *amphorae*) from Spain; wooden wine barrels from Germany; fine lamps and marble ornaments from Italy; and sparkling jewellery from Egypt.

All of these had to be transported in ships. Part of a cargo ship was discovered on the banks of the River Thames in 1910. More recently, in 1962, another vessel was carefully excavated at Blackfriars Bridge, in London. It was a flat-bottomed boat, similar to a barge, that was used to

The cargo ship found by the River Thames in 1910 probably looked like this. It would have been used to bring goods, like oil and pottery, from the Mediterranean.

Sails probably made of linen.

The hull was made of oak. It was about 18 m long and 5 m wide.

Steered by two paddles, one on each side of the stern.

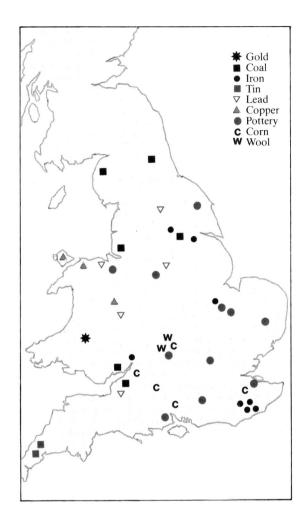

✳	Gold
■	Coal
●	Iron
■	Tin
▽	Lead
▲	Copper
●	Pottery
C	Corn
W	Wool

Iron, copper, silver and lead were mined. At Dolocouthi, in Dyfed, the remains of a Roman gold-mine have been unearthed. Mining took place both above and below the ground, and the entrance to some of the underground tunnels can still be seen. Much of the work in the mines and quarries was tough and dangerous and would have been done by slaves.

LEFT This map shows the location of the main industries set up by the Romans. Making pottery and woollen clothes were the most successful ones.

carry building stones from Kent to the capital until it sank.

As time went on, Britain began to produce many of her own goods, so less had to be imported from other countries. The pottery industry, especially, grew very quickly in Oxfordshire, along the River Nene in Northamptonshire, in the New Forest in Hampshire and in Derbyshire. The kilns that the Romans used to bake the clay, like those found near Castor, in Northamptonshire, were very advanced for their time.

A beautiful glass jug and bowl. They were found in Buckinghamshire.

Religion

Like the Britons, the Romans were pagans – that is, they worshipped many gods. However, their main religion involved the worship of the Roman emperor. A temple to the Emperor Claudius was built at Colchester soon after the invasion. This was a very grand building, much bigger than the temples at which most Romans worshipped in Britain. These were similar to the one that has been found at Wanborough, in Surrey. This was a square, tower-like building, surrounded by a covered walkway, in all 15 m square.

The Romans allowed the Britons to keep their own gods and most of these became linked to Roman ones. We know that one British god, called Taranis, was worshipped at the Wanborough temple.

These pictures, painted by Christians, have been found on the walls of Lullingstone villa.

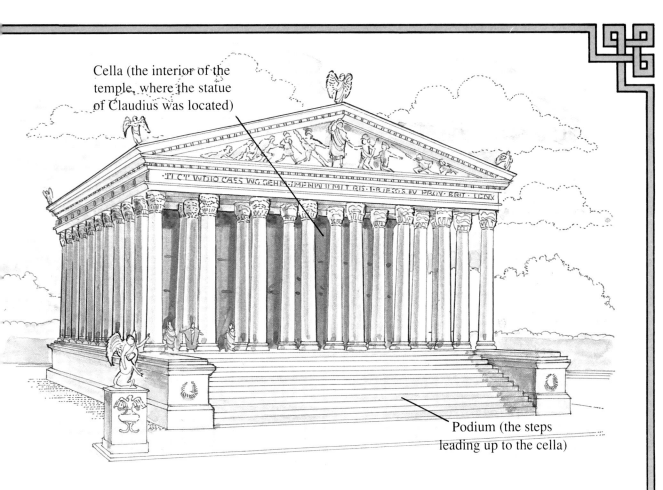

Cella (the interior of the temple, where the statue of Claudius was located)

Podium (the steps leading up to the cella)

The splendid temple in Colchester in which the Emperor Claudius was worshipped.

He became linked with the Roman god Jupiter. Eastern gods, like the Persian one named Mithras, were also worshipped. A temple to Mithras was excavated in London in 1954 (the picture on page 14 shows what it looked like).

At the beginning of the fourth century, the Christian religion was accepted by the Roman Government. Christians had been treated very cruelly until then; now they were able to worship in peace. A building, which is thought to have been a church, has been found at Silchester and a fine mosaic, from the villa at Hinton St Mary, in Dorset, contains a picture of Christ at its centre.

These are the remains of a temple near Carrawburgh, Northumberland, in which the god Mithras was worshipped. The concrete pillars show where wooden posts once stood.

Places to visit

Remains of Roman Britain can be seen at the following places:

Aldborough, North Yorkshire: town.
Baginton (The Lunt), West Midlands: reconstructed fort.
Bartlow Hills, Cambridgeshire: burial mounds.
Bath, Avon: public baths.
Bignor, West Sussex: villa.
Brecon Gaer, Powys: fort.
Caerleon, Gwent: legionary fortress and amphitheatre.
Caerwent, Gwent: fine remains of town walls.
Canterbury, Kent: town house preserved under shopping precinct.
Carrawburgh, Northumberland: fort and temple on Hadrian's Wall.
Chedworth, Gloucestershire: villa.
Chesterholm, Cumbria: fort and reconstructed buildings.
Chesters, Northumberland: fort on Hadrian's Wall.
Chysauster, Cornwall: country village.
Colchester, Essex: Balkerne Gate.
Dolocouthi, Dyfed: gold-mine.
Dorchester, Dorset: amphitheatre and town house at Colliton Park.
Dover, Kent: lighthouse and Painted House exhibition in New Street.
Fishbourne, West Sussex: palace.
Hadrian's Wall, Northumberland and Cumbria.
Housesteads, Northumberland: fort.
Leicester, Leicestershire: Jewry Wall.
London: town wall.
Lullingstone, Kent: villa.
Maiden Castle, Dorset: British hillfort and Roman temple.
North Leigh, Oxfordshire: villa.
Pevensey, East Sussex: fort.
Portchester, Hampshire: fort.
Richborough, Kent: fort.
St Albans, Hertfordshire: theatre.
Silchester, Hampshire: town.
South Shields, Tyne and Wear: Arbeia Roman port.
Welwyn, Hertfordshire: bath-house preserved under the A1 motorway.
Wroxeter, Shropshire: town.
York, North Yorkshire: fortress.

Museums
Aldborough, North Yorkshire
Caerleon, Gwent
Canterbury, Kent
Carlisle, Cumbria
Chester, Cheshire
Cirencester, Gloucestershire
Colchester, Essex
Dorchester, Dorset
Gloucester, Gloucestershire
Hull, Humberside
Leicester, Leicestershire
Lincoln, Lincolnshire
London: British Museum and Museum of London
St Albans, Hertfordshire
Winchester, Hampshire

Glossary

Amphitheatre An open-air, oval-shaped building with a central area surrounded (by seats, where entertainment took place.

Archaeologist A person who studies ancient remains found in the ground or under water.

Ballista A type of large crossbow.

Barracks A building where soldiers live.

Basilica The long building down one side of the forum.

Bastion A tower which sticks out from the wall of a town or a fort.

Charred Turned black by burning.

Destination The place a person is travelling to.

Fortified A building or place that has been protected from attack.

Furnace A fierce, powerful fire which produces a lot of heat.

Gladiators Men trained to fight in public shows in an amphitheatre.

Granary A building for storing grain.

Hobnails Large-headed nails in the soles of boots to improve their grip.

Import To bring in goods from another country.

Kiln An oven for hardening clay, pottery and tiles.

Mail Armour made out of small metal rings linked together.

Mosaic A picture made out of tiny pieces of coloured pottery and stone.

Ornament Something to make a room look pretty.

Quarry A place where stone is dug out of the ground.

Quay The place where ships tie up in a harbour to unload.

Scales In armour, thin, overlapping pieces of metal.

Shaft The thin, wooden pole behind the tip of an arrow or bolt.

Toga The long, white piece of cloth that the Romans wrapped around themselves.

Books to read

Caselli, G. *The Roman Empire and the Dark Ages* (Macdonald, 1981)

Corbishley, M. *The Roman World* (Kingfisher, 1986)

Cork, B. & Ashman, S. *The Young Scientist Book of Archaeology* (Usborne, 1984)

Embleton, R. & Graham, F. *Hadrian's Wall in the Days of the Romans* (Frank Graham, 1984)

Laing, L. & J. *The Young Archaeologist's Handbook* (Severn House, 1977)

Unstead, R. J. *A Roman Town* (Hutchinson, 1977)

Warner, P. *Roman Roads* (Wayland, 1980)

Wilkins, F. *Growing up in Roman Britain* (Batsford, 1979)

Index